Interwoven

ALSO BY NGOZI OLIVIA OSUOHA

The Transformation Train
Letter to My Unborn
Sensation
Tropical Escape (with Amos O. Ojwang')
Fruits from the Poetry Planet
Poetic Grenade
Whispers of the Biafran Skeleton
Chains
Raindrops
Freeborn
Eclipse of Tides
The Subterfuge
Green Snake on a Green Grass
Chariots of Archangels
Wonderment

Interwoven

a compilation of poems by
Ngozi Olivia Osuoha

Poetic Justice Books
Port St. Lucie, Florida

©2020 Ngozi Olivia Osuoha

Interwoven was compiled from poems previously published in a variety of online venues and Facebook group contests, the fourth such compilation.

book design and layout: SpiNDec, Port Saint Lucie, FL
cover image: *Debate 7*; silver gelatin print, 2009; Kris Haggblom

All rights reserved.

No part of this book may be used or reproduced in any manner whatsoever without written permission except in the case of brief quotations embodied in critical articles and reviews. Members of educational institutions and organizations wishing to photocopy any of the work for classroom use, or authors, artists and publishers who would like to obtain permission for any material in the work, should contact the publisher.

Published by Poetic Justice Books
Port Saint Lucie, Florida
www.poeticjusticebooks.com

ISBN: 978-1-950433-37-7

FIRST EDITION
10 9 8 7 6 5 4 3 2 1

dedication

*In loving memory of all my grand parents, Maazi JOHN ONYECHERE OHIAGU OSUOHA and Oriaku JENNY UKACHI OSUOHA
And
Nze EMMANUEL OZURUMBA AJOKU and Loolo ESTHER IKWUOMA AJOKU*

contents

To Everything There Is a Time 3
Womanhood 4
The German Yam 5
Mum, My Angel 6
Grandma 7
War 8
Live Your Dream 9
A Kind Soul 10
Pink 11
Sands of Time 12
Tolerance 13
Beauty Is Simplicity 14
Live in the Moment 15
Power of Words 16
A Dream Come True 17
Live Fearlessly 18
Optimism 19
Florets of Fancy 20
Joys of Charity 21
Home 22
Family 23
Humility 24
Special Moments 25
Feminism 26
Friendship 28
Autumn Musings 29
Your Smile Is Your Greatest Asset 30
Holy Dove 31
Loved You Then, Love You Still 32
Happy Mothering Sunday 33

Damsel 34
When I Was a Damsel 36
Where Is My Love? 38
Things I Love About You 39
The Essence of Being a Woman 40
Unity in Diversity 41
Everyday Is a New Start 42
Beautiful People Do Not Just Happen 43
Never Say Goodbye 44
Motherland 45
I Have Wings 46
Hopeful Journey 47
Circus 48
When I Look Into My Eyes 49
My Quiver 50
I Will Speak 51
Arise and Shine 52
Wonders of Winter 53
Asia 54

Interwoven

TO EVERYTHING THERE IS A TIME

Let us be swift
For today is a great gift
As God has given us a lift.

Come, gather, and praise our King
Adore God whom causes us to sing
Bring your baskets into His ring
Let those fruits swing, and swing.

Dance, rejoice, blow the trumpet
Raise your voices, and the cornet
Let the heavens enjoy this concert.

Praise the lord, oh our soul
For the lord is in control
And our land has yielded whole.

The harvest is bounty
We have plenty
Let no one come empty.

We planted, we weeded
We waited, we have harvested
He spared us, Us He protected
All glory to the Holy Trinity

WOMANHOOD

It is a crown
You dare not frown
It is a throne
It lasts like bone,
Womanhood, purity of life.

Pride is the clothing
Sincerity, the abode
Dignity is the calling
Respect, the destiny
Virtue is the footpath
Love, the footprints
Womanhood, a vessel of honour.

Culture, tradition and religion
Society, politics and academia
Lift this gorgeous gift
Pamper her to the world beyond,
Womanhood, a gift to mankind.

THE GERMAN YAM

Yam in our barn
Yet, we yawn
The thread and yarn
Festivals yearn.

The German yam
Can run our dam,
But we ruin the hood
And run from good.

Yam in the farm
Shores, the charm
Climes milking arm
Overseas, the harm.

The yam, the German
The German, the yam
Festival of the gods
Beaten with the rods.

A few days from now
We would take a vow
Not with the cow
As we eat the yam
With a ram.

The German yam
Differs from the Nkwerre yam,
Board your bus
Come, dine with us.

MUM, MY ANGEL

I love my mum
She is my angel,
A true beauty
In the face of empty.

She is my queen
Wherever she has been,
She prays for me
And provides for me.

Her calmness in trouble
Her submissiveness
And pureness of heart,
These make me wonder.

I have never seen her kind
A homely teacher,
Dedicated and committed
The wonder of womanhood
And cord of motherhood.

GRANDMA

True African woman
Humble and poor,
Uneducated but wise
Local but sophisticated.

Down to earth
Contented and satisfied,
Hopeful and faithful.

Cheerful, tolerant
Hearty, elegant
Industrious and strong.

Prayerful, beautiful
Wonderful, amazing
Caring and loving.

Always there, within and without
Always here, now and then
Heart, body and soul.

Complete with a world
Adored and chosen
Cute in a scene
Beyond this serene.

Missing you, everyday
Day by day
But yet never gone.
IN MEMORY OF JENNY UKACHI OSUOHA

WAR

O foolish war
You killed peace
And butchered unity
What hast thou gained?

O violence
You raped love
And tortured care
What hast thou gained?

O terror
You razed heaven
And burnt earth
What hast thou gained?

Hold thyself
Keep the peace
War no more
This fight is cruel
Give peace a chance.

LIVE YOUR DREAM

The world is so fake and ridiculous
Everything hectic and rigorous
But one can be fulfilled
Only by living one's dream.

Live your dream
If you want to be happy
Live your dream
If you want to be great,
Live your dream
If you want to be rich.

Greatness is not riches
Riches are not greatness
Fulfilment is life
Life is a legacy.

Footprints, footpaths, footsteps, footmarks
All, are traces, traces of who lived.

A good name is better,
Goodwill is awesome
The future matters most, yesterday is gone
Today, is a ladder, timely climbing and right rung
Dreams become realities.

Dreamers are insane, insane dreamers rule
Live your dream, drive your train
Power your turbine, the locomotive is unique
Tour the world, enjoy your ride
For living is transitory.

Ngozi Olivia Osuoha

A KIND SOUL

A kind soul is unique
Does not mess around,
He is genuine, real and courageous
His love is contagious,
No strings, no ulterior motives
No gains in pursuit
A kind soul just helps.

He is not dangerous
Though his skin be cancerous
He is not deadly
Though his appearance is poor
A kind soul is divine
His benevolence is outstanding.

A kind soul is a gift
He lives to lift
His feet are swift
To lift from the rift,
A kind soul is a blessing
He is natural and raw.

You can be a kind soul
Yes, you can save the lost world
You can heal the sick world
Yes, you can mend the brokenhearted,
A kind soul, we can be.

PINK

I am pink
I stand tall against all odds.

I am pink
I sail, I float
The sea is mine.

I am pink
I bud, I grow
My petals open
I spread like other flowers.

I am pink
I rule the lettuce
And order their circle.

I am pink
I love green
I love flowers
The water harbours us.

SANDS OF TIME

A life lived in waywardness is gone
Totally gone and empty,
What is life if lived waywardly?

A life in laziness is unfruitful
Unfruitful and empty,
What is life if lived in the wind?

Young or old, black or white
Rich or poor, male or female
Make history, create history
Discover, explore, invent, innovate
Write your name in the sands of time.

Write it well, make it bold
Engrave it, inscribe it, print it
Mark your name loud
Let nothing clean it when you are gone.

TOLERANCE

Tolerance is the key
Because the world has gone nuts
Religion plants discord
Racism sows disunity
We scatter, shatter and batter.

We can live in peace
If we understood each other
And accept our differences,
If we build on our gaps
And work on our similarities,
Tolerance is all we need.

Talents, gifts, goals and dreams
Visions, hopes and aspirations
Zeal, courage and missions
Far and wide, near and without
Tolerance gears our passion.

Fanaticism and extremism
Lust and hate, pride and supremacy
All can be guided, guarded and curtailed.

BEAUTY IS SIMPLICITY

The world is a stage where actors perform
And the audience cheer according to performance.

The world is heavy and full of issues
So humans roll along with life,
They play the way they choose or forced to
So sometimes, they regret their actions.

However, simplicity is the beauty of life
That way one tends to stand firm
Wise decisions, brilliant choices, distinct tracks
Proper guidance, self control, self esteem and respect
Focus, determination, zeal, hope and prayers
These and many more align one to success.

Beauty is simplicity, simplicity is beauty
Prudence, diligence, dedication and commitment
One lives simple, simply, simplified and satisfied.

LIVE IN THE MOMENT

Time is a slippery phenomenon
It waits for no one, even itself,
Tomorrow never comes
And if it does, it stares at you
Prepare today, for tomorrow
Live in the moment.

Live as if tomorrow will never come
Pay your dues to life
Keep your friends real
Leave legacies that are indelible
Print bold your footprints, tiny or big
Make your path broad and loud
It is your duty to maintain your footsteps.

Life is a passage
Crazy, the world is
We follow it to the one, yonder
Never be a noise
Echo your voice, let it reverberate
Raise your tune, tone and frequency.

Let the moments be monumental
Crystal, golden, and dazzling like diamond
For nothing is ever guaranteed tomorrow.

Ignore the winds, fight the storm
Let your dream be the wave
Live in the moment!

Ngozi Olivia Osuoha

POWER OF WORDS

The earth was created by words
Since then, words have been active.

The tongue is tiny but red
It bears flames and fires
It could spark, it could burn.

Words heal, words hurt
Words expose, words conceal
The power of words are indescribable.

Soft words melt anger
Harsh words ignite fury,
Tender lines pierce hearts
Strong pages raze homes.

Words are powerful
They go a long way
They build, they scatter
They unite, they shatter
Words are gods
They are invisible but incredible.

A DREAM COME TRUE

I have always wondered the chances
The chances of being an author,
Due to circumstances and situations.

I have always doubted
Doubted the possibilities of being published,
The dream of touring the world.

Yes, I had prayed, longed and hoped
I was disappointed and discouraged
I was downcast, downtrodden and confused.

The ups and downs, highs and lows
Fears and doubts, lacks and necessities
Wants and needs, boredom and loneliness
But here am I today, a published author.

I am a poet, writer and thinker
I have published seven poetry books and coauthored one
With over two hundred and fifty poems and articles
Published in over twenty countries.

Yes, I have also featured in over forty international anthologies
Uncountable works in progress,
Numerous dreams coming true and through
I cannot believe it would be this tremendous.

Published mostly overseas, winning awards
Hoping for brighter days, pushing and praying
Though not rich, but money is not everything
Legacies upon legacies, printing in the sands of time.

A footpath and footprint so eligible
Happy, proud, contented, grateful
It is just a dream come true.

LIVE FEARLESSLY

Fear is a spell
It dries your well,
Fear is a bullet
It kills the millet.

Fear is a beast
It poisons the feast,
Fear is a weapon
It harms the coupon.

Live fearlessly
Fight faithfully
March fearlessly
Fight faithfully.

Life is a war
Everything is raw,
Life is a law
Everything is a saw.

Fear blinds, it nothing finds
Doubt is a demon, it all does summon
So you are a Simon,
Lift your Simeon
And live the sermon.

See, life is green
Been, seen, or green
Plant it, water it, weed it
Harvest time shall be glorious.

Live without a fear
Tear the bear, and wear your gear
Clear your ear, hear my dear
Near the rear, tear the frightening wear.

OPTIMISM

The world is no longer sane
And none is on their lane
They spared the rod and cane
And burnt the sugarcane.

No more integrity
Lost and gone is sincerity
No more honesty
Abhorred is authenticity.

Trust is a trap
Obedience is a crap
Love is a scam
Unity is to harm.

Terrors and wars
Violence and atrocities
No hiding place, no fortress
Nothing is exempted, nor safe.

However, I am optimistic
Our God shall come in great might
To restore the dignity of man,
The peace of His creation.

FLORETS OF FANCY

Beautiful sight they do display
Colours like that of the rainbow
Red, orange, yellow, green, blue, indigo, violet
Scents of enchanting fragrance.

Florets of fancy down the valley
Purple headed mountain up above
Meadows and springs calm and serene
Birds and butterflies thirst no more.

Serenades of lovely parades
Warding off masquerades of ugly shades
Florets of fancy are divine
Tranquility in unison.

JOYS OF CHARITY

Charity begins at home
But sometimes, home is far away.

The poor needs help
A helping hand of charity,
So the poor could be home.

The sick needs healing
Healing from wounds, ailments
So the sick could be home.

When we help, we save
When we give, we preach
When we rescue, we build
The joy of giving is tremendous.

Giving too is a gift
Not all have it
It is better to give than receive
For blessed is the hand that gives.

Divine joys radiate
Fountains of joy flow in hearts
Hearts that do charity.

Give therefore, it shall be given unto you
Good measures shaken together and running over.

HOME

Home is god, it is real
It gives comfort and support.

Home is god, it is great
It lifts burdens and cuddles.

Home is god, it is mild
It loves weird and feeds dreams.

Home is god, it is sure
It supplies food and gives strength.

Home is life, it builds future
And anoints life.

Missions and visions, hopes and aspirations
Dreams and realities, wounds and wars
All heal at home.

Home is god, it sustains
Home is breath, breeding and breathing.

Home is all, all is home
Everything, everyone needs a home.

FAMILY

Family is beyond bond
It sustains like pond
And makes us to be of each other, fond
Family dresses and addresses.

Family is beyond blood
It stays afloat the flood,
Family is a shrine
It makes all fine,
Family is a vine
It produces many wine
Male, female, pets, livestock
Friends, loving, fighting, giving, taking
Sacrificing, preserving, ending, hoping
Family, is a link beyond what we drink.

Support from within, kills hate outside
Home love booms far and wide
Home is god especially when home is good.

HUMILITY

Humility is a rare tool
It helps a great swim in the pool,
Humility is a brave guide
It points to you, the tide.

Humble souls attend greatness
Proud beings meet shame,
Humility is a coat
It rescues a sinking boat.

The beauty of humanity
The strength of charity
Humility, a cap of diligence
Sincerity, a crown of patience.

Humility in the struggle
Audacity in the jungle
Nobility in the puzzle
Honesty in the tussle,
Loyalty in the hustle
Humility pays them all.

SPECIAL MOMENTS

We can never forget them
Those moments that make us,
The moments our joys flow
And our happiness abound.

When we are in the arms of our loved ones
When we birth new ideas
When our dreams come true
Yes, those moments when we feel God.

Sweet memories, memories of green life
When a new born visits,
When a new couple becomes
When we arrive peacefully and warmly
When our ambitions meet us.

Yes, those special moments
Moments, so golden
Crystal like stars
So valuable and treasurable like diamonds,
Moments God intervene, erasing protocols on our behalves.

Special moments so divine
When love is embedded in our wombs of time
And trust cultivated in our abode
Those true moments when life seems perfectly beautiful.

Ngozi Olivia Osuoha

FEMINISM

Not toys, play not with us
Not objects, experiment not with us
Our voice is loud, amidst the crowd.

Your manhood is bold
Crystal like a star
Your kingdom is real
Like a cluster of stars.

We plot no coup
We overthrow you not,
Give us love, care and respect.

Feminism is not a war
She does not besiege,
Hearken to her plea.

This plight is necessary
We fight this night
With might to right.

Feminism is not hate nor hatred
It is never bitterness
Embrace the girl child
Lift her from the ashes
Her body is a temple not a laboratory.

Call it frustrations, rages
Name it anger, protest
Tag it rivalry, contest
Theme it what suits you,
Feminism is not a tug of war.

Men too are feminists
Support women, help them
Say no to rape
Cultural and traditional abuse
Trafficking, prostitution and the likes.

Let females be treated fairly, respectfully
Give them peace, peace of mind
Build them, build them up.

FRIENDSHIP

Friends make or mar
They do keep or kill,
So there is need to be Choosey.

Friends come in diverse forms
Some accidentally, coincidentally
Friends solve many problems
As well as create them,
Hence the need to be careful.

Friends speak many languages
We meet them at different times in life,
At birth, at death, in good times, in bad times
Therefore it is important that we understand them.

Friendship is necessary, but not with everyone
Friendship binds, it severs too
It can build tower and raindrops
It can build bridges and raise walls,
Hence we must be vigilant.

Peers, childhood friends, colleagues, role models
Guardians, parents, siblings, relatives, and others
All these have played roles in our lives
Positive, negative, neutral, and lots more
However, friends, real friends encircle as family.

AUTUMN MUSINGS

Like autumn, we shed leaves
Leaves of musings, musings of ink
Ink, inking nature.

Beauty fades, yes it does
As leaves shed, the shade empties
Getting ready to build up better.

Nature, cool and calm
Quiet, breezy, windy and friendly
Pure, poor and rich.

Autumn musings, musings of the gods
Fortifying the grounds, enriching the soil
Gathering manure for the fall.

Giving ants more rooms to store up
Birds of the air, taking peaceful flights
Autumn musings, rich, dry and real.

YOUR SMILE IS YOUR GREATEST ASSET

Life is not rosy, nor greenish
We burn like fire and our flames go up
Everywhere is hot, and everything is boiling
No peace, no love, no trust, no safety
It is as if we all are mad,
But one can smile amidst the storm
Because your smile is your greatest asset.

Nothing is guaranteed, wears and tears
Nothing is permanent, even gold and silver
Wealth vanishes, health diminishes
But in all one can smile
Because your smile is your greatest asset.

Smile in the storm, smile at the storm
Smile for the storm, smile through the storm
Smile, just keep smiling, for life is tough
Smile until it gets tired of upsetting you.

Your smile is your greatest asset
Never think otherwise
Because all other assets are perishable.

HOLY DOVE

White, clean and neat
Holy, pure and sacred
Come, holy dove
Visit this burning world
And quench its flames.

Return, lost peace
Come, live in our midst
Dwell beyond our comprehension
Let no man trouble you again.

Descend from above
Speed forth in might and glory
Chase away waves of war
And tides of disasters,
Still the earth, calm the spirits
Reign, reign, holy dove.

Peace, peace, be ours
Hate, greed, racism, be gone
Slavery, terrorism, be lost
World, world, be calm.

Ngozi Olivia Osuoha

LOVED YOU THEN, LOVE YOU STILL

Loved you then, love you still
You were my star, my light
You were my rose, my love
You were my peace, my calm
Yes, loved you then, love you still.

You are my pride, my confidence
You are my joy, my happiness
You are my wealth, my health
Yes, loved you then, love you still.

Thorns tore my flesh, you stitched them
Sorrows boiled my heart, you cooled me
Hunger burnt my passion, you ignited me
I loved you then, and I still do.

You are real, faithful and compassionate
You are pure, true, lovely and caring
Your heart is a field, your soul, heaven
Your body is a vegetation, you are fertile
I loved you then, I will love you more.

When I lacked, you provided
When I needed, you came around
When I wanted, you cushioned
You are love, my love, my true love
I will love you still, because I loved you then.

HAPPY MOTHERING SUNDAY

The pillar of great support
With the strength of a deity
Charming the universe
Igniting her passion.

Bold, brave and courageous
Smart, unique and outstanding
True, real and articulate.

The world heeds to your voice
She rotates on your love,
Today, we speak to creation
And beseech her coasts to enlarge
That all may celebrate your feat.

Let the north, south, east and west
Open their hands in memorial
For you, yours, yours and thine.

Happy mothering Sunday
Happy Heroes' Day
Cupid, we bow for you this day.

DAMSEL

Beautiful damsel, soft and succulent
Growing like the pride of Barbados
Green, young and lively
Dreams bloom in you.

A damsel of great world
From a marvelous God
To do tremendous things
Look, the world beckons.

May life be peaceful with you
May it show you kindness,
May troubles keep their claws off you
That you explore adventures.

O lovely damsel
A gift to mankind
A picture of heaven,
Bloom, boom and blossom
That we know love undiluted.

When you work the lanes of life
And drive the roads of beauty
When you fly the routes of wisdom
And beyond paddle the waves of need,
When you row the sea of choice
And run the race of hunger,
May you see divine directions.

Little damsel, an epitome of future
Grow and dazzle for the world to see
Glitter more than gold
And shine your light,
Twinkle like stars
And enlighten the world.

Cheerful damsel, calm creation
Look away from whirlwind and hurricanes
Stay away from landslides and earthquakes
They could be manmade too.

Never stay off course
Focus on your mission
 By the time you grow up
The world would have learnt from you.

Ngozi Olivia Osuoha

WHEN I WAS A DAMSEL

When I was a damsel
I lived in fantasies,
I thought life was straight
I danced with the future.

When I was a damsel
I was proud for the future
Because I hoped for the best.

When I was a damsel
I cherished prophecies
And waited for dreams.

When I was a damsel
I believed all must be well,
Because I knew nothing.

But now, I am an adult
A little experience
A little reality,
Facts, truths, bursting myths
It has dawned on me
That life is not about fairy tales.

When I was a damsel
I never knew damsels die
I thought they must live
I thought they must grow
I knew not they could be harmed.

When I was a damsel
I didn't know the world was cruel.

Poverty, hunger, hate, and crime
Rape, war, religion and politics
Unemployment, hunger and lust
Betrayal, gossip, scandals, and slanders
Greed, envy, jealousy and selfishness
Looting, killings, murder and injustice
All these and more proved me wrong.

When I was a damsel
I thought life was peaceful.

Ngozi Olivia Osuoha

WHERE IS MY LOVE?

I am wondering where he is
The one that will guide me
And rule my heart,
The one that will love me
And bless my soul,
The very one that will bring me peace.

I wonder and ponder
I imagine far and deep
I bless his journey and path
The destination he has chosen
To be here with me.

I hope he conquers time and tide
I hope he arrives on time
Safe, sound, hale and hearty
To love me like my king.

THINGS I LOVE ABOUT YOU

Do not ask the things I love about you
Because I love everything about you
Your skin, your hair, your simplicity
Your courage, your honesty, your truthfulness
You are so real and natural
And that holds me together.

Let me tell you more
You make due with what you have
And live within your means
You are so down to earth and polite
Your attitude in a fake world is captivating.

Your imperfections are only human
And I love them, I love you for them.

Your forgiving spirit and friendly manner
Your aura is so encompassing
You are a spell cast upon me
The light that turns off my doubt
I love you just the way you are.

Money and beauty fade
Character is everything
Wealth and health change
Integrity is the sole of life
You and just you make me want to live.

Ngozi Olivia Osuoha

THE ESSENCE OF BEING A WOMAN

I am a god, I rule the world
I make men, I create life
I care, love and procreate,
I am the handiwork of God.

I am a deity, men adore me
I feed the world and replenish the earth,
I am the beauty of life, the essence of love.

I came from the rib of man
I am his missing rib,
I am his flesh, his bone
I am his lover, his keeper, his soulmate
And that's my essence.

I can ruin him, I can build him
I can lift him, I can crush him
I am a god, a deity
I am extraordinary.

UNITY IN DIVERSITY

Culture is dynamic
But we are angelic,
When life is tragic
We can be realistic,
Because anything, barbaric
Can hinder something, gigantic
Even against the public
But in unity
We can stop enmity
And win stupidity
For our diversity
Is a blend of creativity.

Ngozi Olivia Osuoha

EVERYDAY IS A NEW START

Life is full of complexity
And humans display curiosity,
Nature calls them to maturity
But they wander in anxiety,
Looking down on sincerity
And discarding intensity,
However, there is a superiority
That counters their inferiority,
So in the spirit of celebrity
They forget priority
Hitherto, life is a university
Coupled with adversity
And diversity
We forget audacity
And commit atrocity
It is really a pity
How chastity
Offers reality
That everyday is a new start.

BEAUTIFUL PEOPLE DO NOT JUST HAPPEN

Beauty is inbuilt, it is within
The physical is a deceit
Beautiful people have amazing spirit
That is what makes them excellent.

Beautiful people may not have money
But they are rich and willing to give
They are generous even with nothing
These people value life and love.

Sometimes, beautiful people do not just happen
We pay some due to let them shine,
Their heart is golden, pure and free
Nothing stains them no matter who hurts them.

These people hardly complain, they flow like water
Taking the shape of the container
They may be tattered, shattered or haggard
Yet, their mind is the dwelling place of God.

NEVER SAY GOODBYE

Life is great
It can be tough or rough
So let's drive and thrive.

Life is real
It can be up or down
So let's try and fly.

When it is high or low
When it is big or small
When it is front or back
When is deep or shallow
Let's be there, stay put.

Never say goodbye
I need you, you need me
We need us, each other
Just hold on, life is just like that.

A little while, it will be fine
A little more strength, it will pass
Stay strong, hope great
Tomorrow is looking good.

MOTHERLAND

Fertile motherland, pure waters of green fruits
Flowing with milk and honey, land of our ancestors
The bosom of our peace and love
The pride of our dream and vision
How are the mighty fallen!

Dear motherland, the bedrock of our hope
Impatiently swinging, imbalanced and immoral
Who bewitched you to slaughter yourself
That there is no hope for your unborn?

O mighty mother, your land is bruised and broken
Littered with skulls and splintered flesh
No one wants to love you anymore.

Poor mother, the widow of unknown soldier
And lover of unborn children,
How do you manage your shame?

I HAVE WINGS

I have wings, wings of love
I have wings, wings of peace
So I can fly, fly to the ends
I can fly, fly, around the world.

I have wings, wings of life
I have wings, wings of justice
I can fly, fly above the world
To give that which God ordians.

I have wings, wings of tolerance
I have wings, wings of patience
I can fly, fly beyond the earth
To share all that God inspires.

I have wings, wings of freedom
I have wings, wings of courage
I can fly, fly within planets
To distribute what God has in store.

I have wings, wings of unity
I have wings, wings of encouragement
I can fly, fly all over the world
To create calm and tranquil.

O my wings, wings of healing
O these wings, wings of divinity
Fly up and down, far and wide
Heal the hurting, heal the land.

HOPEFUL JOURNEY

Life is a journey, so let us embark on it
For the world is beautiful
And the earth wonderfully made
The sky, the sea, the cloud, the heavenly bodies
All, speak hope and greatness.

Let us live like heroes
Even in this voyage of discovery
Because we shall become great.

The brightness breeds hope
Telling of a future so wondrous,
O this journey of ours, we live it.

Hunger, loneliness, wear and tear
Need, want, lack and plight
Fear, doubt, worry and wishes
We bury them in our journey.

CIRCUS

Hello little children
Today is your fun
Come let us travel round the city
Saint Nicholas is here,
Your favourite saint to gift you all.

Hello, little children
Come, come, come along
Jump up and down
Clap your hands
Look, we have dancers
And storytellers
Listen, listen, we are travelling.

The pussycat, the puppet, the parrot
You can touch and play with them,
We are going on a sightseeing
A tour of fun with sweet drinks and chocolates.

Come along, come along
Join the train, sing with me
The party is on the move.

WHEN I LOOK INTO MY EYES

The mirror is amazing
It gives me a reality
The reality of my being,
So when I look into my eyes
I see wonders.

There is a giant in me
A lion, so untamed
A queen, so great
An angel, so godly
When I look into my eyes
I see God doing wonders.

My eyes are brown and black
They colour the earth
My eyes are blue and purple
They beautify the world.

When I look into my eyes
I see future, peace and love
I see unity and freedom,
Look into my eyes
You will see greatness.

Ngozi Olivia Osuoha

MY QUIVER

I have a quiver
I wear it like a sack
Always on my back.

My quiver is big and great
Strong and long
Heavy and brave.

My venom, my arrows
My ink, my paper
My Bible, my hymnbook
My food, my water
All, are contained therein.

I am a soldier, a warrior
I am an Amazon,
I fight daily, I care not if I lose
This struggle is real
And I have to survive.

If I shiver, with my quiver
If I hunger, with my quiver
If I sleep, with my quiver
If I die, with my quiver
The jungle, made the quiver permanent.

I WILL SPEAK

For all the atrocities in the land
And the killings,
For the blood they shed
And the peace they pieces
I will speak up
I am a poet
A writer from above
I ink my pain, sadness and joy
I shout against evil
I beckon for love
And pray for unity
So I will speak.

They trade with us
And threaten our voice,
They thread through us
And threaten us
I must speak.

The land is ungodly
Humans are beasts
Blood become fountains
Vultures merry daily
I have to speak.

ARISE AND SHINE

Damsel, handmaid of God
I have heard your cry
And seen your tears,
I know your sorrow
And your shame,
The darkness is overwhelming
And this loneliness is suffocating
Rise up and go home
Rise and rejoice
For your light has come,
Listen, I am the holy dove
The spirit of the most high God
Weep no more, cry no more
Wipe your tears, your joy has come
For now is the dawn of your happiness.

WONDERS OF WINTER

O the wonders of winter
As they litter
Scattering across the earth,
Cold, everything so cold
Shivering sometimes.

Deep sleep, better rest
Warm and warmness from heater
Coverings of proper clothing
Warding off cold and coldness.

Snow, mist, dew, fog
Compelling souls on bed
Forcing bodies to sleep longer.

Dry land, hard earth's crust
As vegetations drink little early morning,
Struggles and natural battles
Wanting love and companion,
Wonders of wondrous winter.

ASIA

Asia, the beautiful continent
East of Europe, you are wonderful
Oceania, Arctic ocean, Pacific
You border, and link.

Asia, incredible land
Diverse religions, academic excellence
Beauty and colours, colourful.

Asia, the pride of culture
Traditions rule, norms and values settle
Teeming population, booming people
Lovely, lively, courageous, warm and friendly
Welcoming, hospitality endowed
Knowledge of ancient and modern.

Asia, Asian, Asians,
Continent, person, people of great valour
The land of rainbow soil.

Interwoven

Ngozi Olivia Osuoha is a Nigerian poet, writer and thinker. A graduate of Estate Management with experience in Banking and Broadcasting.

She has fifeen poetry books published in Kenya, Canada, the Philippines, USA, and others. She has also co-authored one (with Kenyan literary critic Amos O. Ojwang').

She has been featured in over sixty-five international anthologies and also has published over two hundred and fifty poems and articles in over twenty countries.

Many of her poems have been translated and published into other languages, including Spanish, Russian, Romanian, Polish, Khloe, Farsi, and Arabic, among others.

She has won many awards; she is a one time *Best of the Net* nominee, and she has numerous words on marble.

colophon
Interwoven, by Ngozi Olivia Osuoha,
was set with Trebuchet MS fonts
by SpiNDec, Port Saint Lucie, Florida
The jacket and covers were designed by
Kris Haggblom, Port Saint Lucie, Florida

www.ingramcontent.com/pod-product-compliance
Lightning Source LLC
Chambersburg PA
CBHW030103100526
44591CB00008B/255